Love

Stories of messages

Crosses

from people and pets

Over

who have died

And a couple of poems

By Elizabeth Allen

LOVE CROSSES OVER

ISBN-9781490547794

Author: Elizabeth Allen

This book is a work of non-fiction.

Printed in the U.S.A.

With all that I am,
and all that I have yet to become,

I dedicate this book to

*F*iona

~ All great truths go through
three stages
First they are ridiculed
Then they are opposed
Then they are accepted as
self-evident ~

Table of Contents

Loss gets fabricated in the telling
Allow it be just for feeling then
As the thorn to the rose
The storm to the wind
Water to tears
No separation shall be known

ELIZABETH

Forward

Only people who are capable of loving strongly can also suffer great sorrow, but this same necessity of loving serves to counteract their grief and heals them.   *Leo Tolstoy*

As a professional animal communicator and spiritual medium, I have contacted those, of both fur and flesh, on the other side. I have been the mediator between the grieving and those who have transitioned into spirit, giving messages that allow for that salty mixture of tears, the source of which comes only from the depth of both comfort and sorrow.

As a person who has consciously and spiritually experienced my own life, I have lived grief, I have felt sorrow, I have loved, I have lost, I have wept, I have healed. In those experiences, and more, Elizabeth Allen and I are soul sisters on a level that transcends common thought.

I work with many people who are at a crossroads of how and when to let go and help their fur-family die with dignity. Elizabeth states it beautifully when she explains, "...*even when you think you've told them a million times that it's ok to go, they seem to know if that is in actuality the truth or just rhetoric. They read the language of the heart perfectly.*" Elizabeth's take on life, love and loss allows the reader to look into the soul of grief and emerge on the other side with an understanding of spiritual acceptance.

It is the true eventuality of the experience of death that all souls in the universe share. How we look at death, spirituality and the process of grieving is how we differ … and how we grow, if we chose to do so. Elizabeth has provided, through poetry and prose, a raw and unflinching look into her life, her loss, and her process, emerging from cocoon-like darkness, unfolding her wings like a butterfly, lighting on the leaf of spiritual knowledge in the glittering light of the sun.

She takes us through the process of grieving, not with morbidity or oppressiveness, but with honest acceptance she leads us on a journey of insight and hope. She solidifies the understanding that ALL of our loved ones, human and animal alike, never really leave, but look over us in spirit, sending messages of their existence and care, if we are able to open our hearts enough to recognize the signs.

I met Elizabeth just 14 short months after her 'Mam' passed into spirit. As we sat in that little café, sipping our coffee and tea, chatting about our lives, our love for animals, and our thoughts on the universe, she shared with me that she was a writer and a poet. With this book, she shares her life in a way not possible through any lunch, any coffee, or any of the many heartfelt conversations that have ensued between us over the years. She opens up her life in such a way as to help the reader know they are not alone.

With the eloquence of five star dining, she serves us the idea that we are not the only ones who may have had to learn to distinguish the difference between love and pain; we are not the only ones who may have struggled to overcome a personal demon; we are not the only ones who might have questioned what it means to love, and lose, those in our lives who we cannot quite imagine going on without.

As both communicator and healer, I work with animals and people in their darkest hour. I have spoken to those in the process of dying, those in the process of grieving, and those who have made their final journey from this life, shedding their physical clothing, and all that weighs them down. When they reach the other side they are greeted with light and with love, and the ties of that love are never broken.

In this book, Elizabeth bridges the gap between those who might be taking their first steps on this difficult journey, and those with similar professions to my own who, for our own sanity, need to remain somewhat removed at times, so we do not become emotionally flooded with the inordinate amount of grief surrounding us.

Elizabeth provides a prospective which reaches beyond the banal, without alienating those who are not yet ready to take steps into the unknown world of the beyond. She presents the beyond as a reality to be accepted and understood through our personal lens of sorrow, and a forward picture of hope.

Yes, without a deep capability of love, we could not plunge into the depths of such pain and sorrow. Yet, like a breath of fresh air found only by breaching the surface, through the words and poetry of this work, we are cleared to understand that we would never trade the pain we feel, for the true blessing of having those shared experiences with the treasured people and animals in our lives.

Lisa Larson
Animal Communicator/Spiritual Medium
Carlsbad, California
2013

~ Do not wait for the animal to find you
Search them out
For faith without action dies
And animals can't drive ~

Myself

Well it's broken, it's definitely broken, of that there's no doubt. But it still beats, beats in my chest like a wild animal when it should be at my feet, shattered into a million pieces, never to be pieced back together again or drenched to its rotten core from all the cry-athons. But it's not. The blessed thing is still working – trust me. It defies all laws of any man-made device. So, I can only conclude it is neither made nor understood by man. It's gotta be a piece of God's work.

Over the last four years I've lost, not "can't find" or misplaced, but lost-lost, my parents and three amazing animals – and before that, my best friend – and way back into my early teens, my Nana. I'd hate to define life by loss, but when it keeps happening, you wonder how you can't, because its comparable to nothing and nobody – not one person, teacher, guide, therapist, book, spiritual or religious belief can lessen the magnitude of pain that comes from losing someone we love. Loss has a job and it never, ever fails.

I grew up in Ireland and death is quite the celebration of sorts because, as a population, we seem to be inclined more than some cultures towards great sorrow and lament. So, we try to seize an opportunity to do so whenever we can, justifying our sometimes miserable damp existence. Maybe that is our culture due to our gritty history; people who have experienced great loss over time and come back fighting, fighting foolishly maybe, but fighting. So, in essence, being Irish became the perfect launching pad for becoming a poet, a writer and a survivor of loss and dire weather. But above all, it prepared me for sadness.

My Nana passed when I was fifteen years old. At that age, I didn't know what to do with it except to keep an eye on my Mam. Christmas morning we got the call. Sudden, swift, precise. From that moment on, life became divided in two. I had a feeling even as a young child that it was going to have its way with us and so I thought, it might be prudent of me to make the most of the times in between.

Over the years, through the great joys and deep losses I've experienced, I've found myself inclined towards great sensitivity, emphatically heart-based. And from such a disposition, rather in touch with the magic of signs from God and from souls, both people and animals who have crossed over. These signs have given me great relief and much laughter, happy-sad tears and validation that there is no death, that energies live on and love is everlasting.

Happily in recent years, I've been blessed doing work I love and which I am very passionate about. That has changed with the passage of time on a grand scale to be honest (I flit around a lot), but there has always been a common thread and that is to help others through loss. This I do through writing and through living. I also get to work with people who are getting ready to say goodbye to their beloved animals and who want to have the best journey they can in the final weeks or days. It is through my work that I've shared the stories of hope with them and pay it forward and do what I feel I am here to do.

As a young child I wrote poetry. It saved me from much. As an adult, short stories, more poems and one particular grueling novel. I've found great solace in the written word. It's been my friend when there seemed to be nobody else. So when it came to this topic, I decided it was time to write some of my own stories, combine some I had already written, and drizzle them with a little bit of poetry. I did this in the hopes that anybody out there who has lost a loved one or beloved pet, might find some comfort and peace knowing they are never really gone, and that although we might feel quite lonely at times, we are never really alone.

It must be said, because I am no shrinking violet, that one of my burning desires is for people to entertain the exact opposite of what we've been conditioned to believe. And to believe in the language of the heart above all else because life and living is designed to dilute everything down to judgment and observation, rather than feeling, and that does nothing to honor the life of someone we love. I firmly believe if we give grief its allotted time, some time-out from the pain itself, we will become efficient readers of signs from our loved ones. Signs which let us know that all is well, nothing is lost and we are loved.

They will continue to live on in our hearts, and the heart being the governor of all things, nothing will be left out. Our knowledge of death, as our limited consciousness would have us know it, this by-product of a lack of belief, will expand into a greater awareness of all that we are and are yet to become. And that the heart and the mouth will turn upwards, towards the sun and smile once again.

~ And I asked, what is the cure for disenchantment? ~

Fiona
What a Belief

I don't know what was the saddest part, for it was all so terribly sad – dripping sad, the most saturated day of my life. Not dripping like charisma or like the fat off a turkey or sweat in the folds of a fat person's skin, just immeasurable, sopping wetness. If someone could have manufactured a device to measure sadness, they wouldn't have been able to take my reading for it would have been off the scale. At times that day, it literally felt like I invented sadness itself.

I have a gazillion beliefs. It's just who I have become. And I know a belief is just a thought that we think consistently, which makes a kind of morbid sense to me because my brain is never really switched off. I have failed in over forty-six years to find the switch. Ok, I will give you an example; I believe hiccups make absolute sense; they wake us up; they literally save us from either choking or dying of boredom; and, I also believe in things I cannot see. I forever believe tomorrow is greater than today; that a drastic haircut can save you hundreds of dollars in therapy; that change is the most consistent thing out there; and, that everything is a sign. That in and of itself is a full-time job – hence I am forever gainfully employed. More importantly, I also believe animals are the windows to our soul. Science will tell you to prove it – I ask you to feel it. I ask you to feel the way to your soul, the place where animals guide us.

Fiona found my soul thirteen years ago and left me yesterday. Well, she didn't really leave and it has only taken me less than twenty-four hours later to know this. She was a force of nature. I found her just as easily as cancer did. We tried to turn it away like an unwanted house guest and sever it off like a corn or bunion. We caught it at every turn, trapped it and squeezed it out, only to have it ooze out like jelly in a sandwich a few months later – or however we have come to measure time upon this planet called loss.

In less than twenty-four hours, life has been turned upside down for me. I can only measure it in milliseconds of heartbreak and in the midst of my crippling sadness, have watched my other animals do the same. Eli, the other cat, has become terribly sick; he can barely leave the litter box. Harleigh, my youngest Chihuahua, has resorted to licking his feet till they bleed. And Juno, the eldest Chihuahua, will not leave my lap or sleep.

You see, I always knew they were capable of great things. They have shown me acts of tremendous courage, strength and love over the years and today they just cannot help themselves but fall prey to my ocean of tears and immerse themselves in actions that allow their fear to manifest itself. They don't want me sad. I don't want me sad. I literally don't want me. You see I didn't lose Fiona, my beloved longtime feline companion, I let her go. I made the appointment. I asked for an end to her pain, but little did I know it was just the beginning of mine.

A year of battling cancer with her fades in comparison to twenty-four hours of missing her. A wind blows through my house and touches my face, leaving salt drying into my neck. I feel like cured meat. My animals don't know why I won't stop crying. I don't know if I ever will. Everything I knew before yesterday has vanished and there is nothing, nothing to replace it with. The sadness feels like a foreign object trapped in my skin that tears are trying to ease out.

Fiona took care of me. She took the pieces of my life I allowed fester inside her, where they rotted and decayed. I caused this I tell myself – I did this. She tells me it was her service to me so I could still be here. *To do what,* I ask myself through a haze of tears I feel might corrupt my keyboard. *To do what exactly, to go on, to be healthy, to help others through what I have learnt from her, from them all?*

Maybe, but today I am not so sure. Today, I doubt the existence of anything that does not bear her name, smell of her or have a dozen or so of her long white hairs attached to it. Today I doubt the existence of life itself as she continues to try to assure me through her memory, that there was no sacrifice.

When I awoke today, I thought yesterday was a dream and when that kind thought evaporated like sweat in the non-existence folds of a anorexic's skin, the damn broke once more and the dream world I had awoken from turned into goldfish shapes and got soaked in the rain.

I fail to understand how a corpse gets through a day, when the spirit is broken. How does the internal and external frame hold up? What force steps in and bridges that almighty gap? Well, this is how – it goes from room to room looking for the missing pieces of itself, trying to tape back into place something familiar. Is she just hiding, did she run away, did I imagine her? Christ almighty, didn't she deserve just one more week? Yet I know these are ridiculous questions, because she had stopped eating a week ago and failed to drink water for the last three days. The cancer in her mouth evicted all her teeth on one side and made it quite impossible to do just about anything except breath, and badly at that. The tumor had made its way deep into her face so much so that her left eye teared consistently and she spent the greater part of her day sneezing. But pain meds and antibiotics helped us in a band-aid kind of fashion.

Over the course of our last year, she was my focus. She had to be. And in the mix of all the chaos and concern that a terminal illness warrants, I put the other three in the background, soft and furry but nevertheless canine and feline haberdashery and today I see them once more as their utterly unique selves. Eli – effected and tender; Harleigh – neurotic and delicate; Juno – gentle like canine cotton wool. They lost Fiona too. I forgot that. They were there every step of the way and they never complained about getting fed late, getting less attention, being shoved off the bed in her honor – just so I could have just one more night with her, alone.

I did what I thought was best. That's all I could do. I took her to my chest and never let her go, and I know if I was given the chance again with her, I would do things so very differently. I would have cleaned up my act years ago. But maybe I do have the chance again for the others, maybe I can do things differently – maybe I should.

I told Fiona to send me a sign. Well, we had a few options just so she wouldn't be limited, because I'm not so sure what kind of tools they have on the other side. And knowing how dense we humans can be, I thought I needed quite a few choices. Yet I needed to hear from her. I needed to know that everything I believed without any proof was indeed true; that she was on Rainbow Bridge waiting for me; that she had made her transition peacefully; that she did forgive me; that she was bigger and more powerful on that side than she could ever have been on this. I don't know what is pushing its way up and through me in a bad seed kind of fashion, corrugating my heart in a whole new way. Everything I thought I once knew is gone, every blessed thing, and I have nothing to replace it with. She is gone.

So, after I finally dragged my shoddy remains to the outside world, to take two small dogs with two very swollen bladders out for a very short walk, I found a postcard stuck into my door. Through the snot and tears, I failed to decipher it until I came back inside when I sat down.

The US Postal Service will not deliver mail to my house due to my killer Chihuahuas. Fair enough. So I have a PO Box. The postcard was from my vet. It was addressed to Fiona. It said: *Time flies when you're having fun. Fiona, it is time to schedule your next visit.* And God sent down the rain one more time.

You see, there was a small yellow handwritten sticker on it that said: *Hello from Indiana Street.* I live on Georgia, just a street away. It's a short distance by foot, but immeasurable by any other means. And as I sit here in awe once more at the beautiful, seamless events of life, I hope that Fiona is getting ready to schedule her next visit. This is indeed one of my many, many beliefs.

Fiona's White

I cannot tell the world how I feel
It makes no rotten sense
Everything before and after
Simply decays
It melts

A crooked wicked curve
Eyes slanted towards and around me
How does she do that?

I've garnished this from her
Finally
That whatever I imagined love to be
It was nothing and everything the same

She has taken the worst of me
Leaving what some might define
As my
Best
Yet
And within her everything
I could have done without

My heart is criss-crossed
My insides tormented
My organs slain
Lying in the milky sorrow
Curdled in shame

Never again

F I O N A

How oft those words have been spoken
But I mean this more than my next breath
She has come along and will leave me
In shagging
Tormented
Puss-filled
Regret

This puss I extracted from life
She took from me
Every inch and ounce
Without even a meow
And she
Riddled
Throughout
With decomposed
Expired
Old
me

How does this happen?
How does love conquer even when
Everything around it falls
And fails?

She is still wicked
Thank God
With a slow, crooked smile
That twists my bits and pieces
Into knots of joy
Pierced by the notion
That less is indeed
Less

F I O N A

She pip, pip, pips along
Tenderly white
Sleeping less and gulping air
In a famine of feelings
And a ration of care

Her eye
My heart
They drain
The same
And yet grace is
Only hers

This tremor
I feel
Rattles us both

What else is there
Except
What goes
Back
And
Forth
the most?

Mam
Into 2

Divided in two, that is how she has come to know her life, forever divided in two. And like the almost invisible shards of a broken glass, never fully being swept away – consistent memories of the fragility of life – she is reminded how insane it is to even contemplate that there will never be more. Yet there will be no more gluing them back together for she has come to know herself now quite simply as broken.

Last summer, with two months in France under her widening belt, she spent time with her Mam on two quick trips home. On the last visit, after Lizzy got a dose of the crud, (ailments saved especially for people who lived in damp climates causing a chill of the spirit that defies medical explanation or girls that take up smoking in France for two months – *who knows?),* Mam did quite a bit of sitting beside her bed, coughing plenty, smoking no more, peering out the white nets at the gray summer.

She talked of death quite a bit, of what she wanted, closed coffin and all that stuff – no fuss, no nonsense. It's all rubbish she used to say about everything, all rubbish. Her daughter agreed wholeheartedly, as she looked at the frail frame of a breaking spirit, her heart twisting in a hammock-like fashion, knotting between her ribs, aching for a feeling of home she never knew.

Coming back to this two up, two down, almost six months later without her there to peer out the curtains with was just too much to bear. So no peering would be done this time, just blatant staring. This daughter didn't do things by halves.

Her Mum's bedroom now embalmed; the house decaying like her Mam's body did in six short months, Dad glued to the telly, seeing little, hearing less; the Angelus ringing out to a country sounding like a right slap in the face of loss, the loss of never having said *slan abhaile*.

I missed her by one day, she thought. Planes, people, noise, queues, plastic food, paperless flights, the garbage of life everywhere. And she disinfecting her hands one more time, flying so far knowing so little was waiting for her. Drinking as though self-abuse still promised some healing properties after all these years; stamping her insides with an expiration date – the same one cancer had stamped on her Mam. Could people tell that she was losing her mind over the Atlantic, her heart under their feet? Could people tell anything anymore?

Two weeks of her and Dad now, cleaning out Mam's things; putting them into plastic bags; wondering who would be wearing them next. Emptying out, finding out, never letting go. No, she'd do this and stay in one piece, coiled tightly like her Mam showed her. Angry at times, because you could always get a hold of anger she thought, it slammed nicely into things and people; cut the world up; made it more digestible, while grating at times the organs we needed the most. Sadness was the other way round; it was a bastard of getting hold of us. It sanded down our hard edges and corners.

No today she needed anger to get such a ridiculous job done. She needed to do this for Louise also, for she had taken on the biggest load that the child that never leaves home can get saddled with: How to live with the thought of failing two women she loved dearly?

Later that week, walking down Griffith Avenue getting the medical certificate for this woman who had left without any goodbyes between them, the snow falling all around her uncertain Irish-American feet, looking at it reading her own name – the same and still no tears, no sign of that thing they call grief. Yet snow landing silently on her freckled face, imitating sadness.

She had wondered as a child if her Mam was just too busy to think of a different name for her, as though nine months weren't long enough to be ready for such a disappointment. She had resented it for years until she had just plain stopped. She couldn't allow resentment set in, especially when you lived between two places – never fully belonging to either, never knowing if your real life wasn't shaping up nicely someplace else without you. She knew that would be an open invitation to a malignancy of sorts. One might call this bravery or stupidity. It would never be really clear which one. But on days like today, leaving Ireland felt akin to treason.

If only I could have done one last thing for her, something to ease her pain while still alive she thought – packing away a Mother's life into black trash bags. This should be considered unlawful she thought, as she folded a faded pink cardigan onto a cream silk blouse in a way a baker might place a strawberry on a meringue pie, with equal tenderness but less experience. We're not supposed to find out what is important to them after they leave. Her soft clothes hardly worn, handbag light and used, faded pink purse black from the many openings, the side-pockets with little nonsense, just basic, very basic.

And saving itself for last, a small bottle of perfume she had got for her Mam in France. It had made its way into her hospital bag. She had forgotten about it and even when she bought it she felt silly, as though her Mum would just put it away with other rubbish. It's always been easier to love strangers, she thinks. Their actions mean nothing.

With the weight of the finality of everything touching down upon her, she lay down on her Mum's bed, feeling the disappearing light of a woman she didn't know infuse her own brittle body. The world that now remained, swam into a multitude of colors and angels sent down the rain. Inhaling the scent of childhood and loss, the two the same, sleep finally brought her Mam to her.

As clear as day she stood beside her bed, the bed she took her last breath in, dressed in a pink nightdress, soft light like marshmallow fluffing out all around her. Lizzy put on clean sheets, making sure to tuck in the corners perfect and tight, just like she liked them. She gently eased her Mam in under them, looking breakable like the china figurines she loved to decorate the house with. She was like an old photograph that time had bleached most of the color out of but none of the memory. Mother and Daughter together, holding hands, smiling, patting each others' faces, saying nothing, feeling everything worth feeling, nothing left unsaid, passing only love back and forth like a celestial beach ball. And Elizabeth reached up with the hands only a Mother possessed to her daughter's face, and with a gentleness she had never really known or felt while alive said, it's time to let me go now Lizzy, it's time. And so she did, she did that one last thing.

She's back again, trying to coexist between two worlds, divided always divided; sliced by the workings of life and assured of the precision of loss. And wondering of the possibility of a minor restoration of a culinary raw heart, or just wondering at the foolishness of such a thought. And she remembers the man she met on the plane, the man who had lost his Mammy too. This complete stranger that looked in her eyes and told her that there was no getting over such a thing and how she loved and hated him all at the very same time.

I wrote this quite soon after my Mam's death. It helped me heal. And I know now that my Mum gave me something I will never ever forget. A visit. What I didn't say in the story was that when I fell asleep that day, I felt as though I had been shot through space and time, a tunnel of sorts. If you've seen *Back to The Future*, it was exactly like that. I held on as I was blasted down a tube at light speed, colors flashing everywhere, holding on with my life to the invisible sides, yet feeling safe in letting go of everything, including thought itself.

If I could remember being born, I'd have to say this must be the same feeling – the feeling of being shot out into her bedroom, into the white light like nothing I have ever known before. It was as close to God as I can imagine being – the source of love, for that was all I felt. And as soon as the scene was over, I was shot right back into the room and plopped back on her bed. And I thought to myself, nobody is ever going to believe me.

But today I know I was wrong. I'm not alone in such an experience. I've had others and I hope I might have more someday. It's like a time-out from life – and no yoga, meditation, sleep, green smoothie, self-help group, spiritual book or detox weekend has even come close.

GO softly

Go softly she said
Go softly into the sun
Right into the center
And I will meet you there

We have made it
We have made it a little bit
Not what it was
Nor not what it was supposed to be
We have made it
What it is
Not what it forever shall be

Who am I?
Who do I want to be?
I cannot become that which I am supposed to be
Until I stop being that which I am not

And I am not that which you see
I am that which I am having trouble being
And seeing
I am becoming

Mam Again
The Kettle

Mam has come to visit me in a glorious mixture of remembrance of colors and smells. She smells of pink gold and Motherhood. It's very distinct. There's no mistaking it. In prayer or meditation when I ask to connect with her, she's there but over time she had to fly off you see. She had to go with those demanding angels, though I would have been happy to have her spirit close to me always (I'm a terribly selfish daughter). But she needed to heal also and celestial healing takes time and doesn't do so well with bothersome daughters checking in. Funny thing all the same, trying to keeping spirits close and for ourselves – I've come to find out they also need time alone and my Mam's spirit was no exception.

About a year into her passing, I'd hit an emotional roadblock. I couldn't breathe without inhaling her, wanting her close and it didn't feel quite healthy. So I opted for some healing and during a deep meditation I was guided by a teacher to let her move on. She said "If you keep running your Mum's energy there will be nothing left of you." Part of me didn't care if there was. But nonetheless I had gotten myself here and I knew it was best for everyone if I tried to move beyond it. Yet to be honest, I'd quite gotten used to having a foot in both worlds. It suited my disposition well – but like a cork in the bottle that prevents breathing, something had to be dislodged if I was to live fully in one. So I closed my eyes and allowed myself be walked through it, fearful I wouldn't get to feel her ever again. But I knew as long as I kept opening the wound of loss, it wouldn't have a chance to heal, fully.

When I finally settled into my meditation, I saw myself and Mam on the beach walking, her wrist tied to mine with a red thread, the color of deep love. We felt the sand between our feet as we walked, not talking, sending love back and forth once again in an authentically effortless fashion. I turned to her and was told to cut the thread. With tears in my eyes, I severed the string, kissed her powdery face and began to walk away. It felt like a miscarriage of minor injustices.

My heart pumped sadness in every direction, my pulse reached unclockable speeds as tears ran down my face, turning to salt in the wind – understanding the need for separation but not being as strong as I needed to be. I turned to give Mum one last glance and told her I would be ok. Like all Mothers do, she hesitated, she would have stayed but with her red string falling to the ground, a flock of angels swooped down and scooped her away like precious celestial cargo. They had been waiting for her patiently, waiting to take her to a resting place where she too could go and heal. And as I came back to my body, sitting in my damp reality, I had a vague feeling I would be ok.

After that healing, I felt a shift. Mam wasn't around anymore, but I knew I had a forever access pass to her should I need one. I felt she was on the mend also and that if I should want to connect with her she would make herself known to me. So about a year later, when I had conveniently forgotten my promise to her, I tried again and this is what transpired.

I was in the kitchen, frustrated after a long and painful meditation that seemed to yield nothing for me. Sometimes they're like that, indifferent, like a mediocre workout when you know staying home eating old M&M's, watching reruns on telly would have been a better choice. Yet as exciting as it sounds, I was trying to test my spiritual waters, so to speak. I had almost finished my first six months of clairvoyant training and not feeling very authentic about it, but trying to complete it nonetheless. I was frustrated by my lack of experience, cursing just about everything and believing in very little beyond my average, uncultivated five senses.

The kitchen was lit by a dim night light, my arms tightly crossed over my chest, as I continued to berate myself, my lack of experience and multiplying impatience. Super-natural my arse! There was nothing super about this and nothing about it felt in any way natural. Why not show me a sign then, I asked my Mam? What's it to you anyway? Don't tell me you don't have time, I offered up. You've got all the time in the world and beyond. Come on Mam, I need to feel you today. Where in God's name are you? Busy? Aaaarrgh!!!

I love tea. I drink it by the gallon. It's also part of my national heritage. Everything in life gets solved with a cuppa – everything. Our kettle boiled itself dry a million times a day growing up. We bonded over tea and toast like nobody's business, even during times of strife. It is what glued us together when we wanted to kill each other. After tea, we'd think, after tea I'll throttle her. Tea was a whole other religion and it saved many a family.

So I glanced at the kettle, which was made of glass so I could see it was empty across the kitchen. That would never have been the case in Ireland. But as I stood there contemplating filling it for a midnight cuppa, irritated by my childishness, the kettle switched on and began to boil itself dry. I walked over, tears making their way for the millionth time down my freckled face, turned it off and went to bed, wrapped in the scent of childhood and tea.

My Mam was a force while alive and in spirit she was no less. Today though, I've stopped asking my Mam for signs. At least it feels like ages ago since I needed one, but I'm most assured should I change my mind, which I am known to do, that all I would have to do is ask. And even so after almost five years, there are days I find myself gripped by the invisible hand of grief that seems to appear from nowhere and tighten itself around my heart, whereby I find myself planning the most simplest of things like a trip to the bathroom as though a shower would be worthy of a medal and all the steps in-between.

The Law of shapes

Where have they gone
Those dark shoes, those threadbare laces?
With a hand over cotton, over heart, over heat
I move into memory, for in reality I am but once a year
And I sink into my damp childhood
Which has melted onto those gray suburban streets

Would she have known that along I would come -
She would never have been ready
Too long for too little
She has touched my rough edges, my sharp places
Planting something old and strange
Far and close to love

Yet here I can be found stealing life
Out of her sight
This is but only a false freedom
For as long as there is time we are bound
To this conspiracy of love
That leaves me distrustful of the language of organs
Before my second breath
I completed a dead-end search for signs of pleasure in sanity
Would one think I should be dying to have had such incredible
frivolity while living,
with words, thoughts and deeds?

There is but an inch of her in every move
Yet it is by and far enough
She fed me sad words that steered the majority of me this way
I pray into the night and without her knowing or moving away
I swim beside her, where I slip imperfectly into her crescent
shape
And a sigh escapes from a century's work
Defying the law of shapes

Sinead
Dublin Street

S inead was my best pal. We flitted around the streets of Dublin like two noisy young hooligans, doing what young girls do, getting into trouble. We were as close as two friends could be. We shared everything, clothes, music and yes, sometimes even boys. But most of all, we shared a piece of our life with each other, although we didn't know at the time, it would only be six short months.

I'd known Sinead in school, though not by association. I was quiet. She was not. She made a lot of noise over the years, giving the nuns quite the run for their calling. I admired her from afar, blown away at her shenanigans, knowing I stood no chance at even an introduction let alone friendship. No, I would sit there looking on for it was not in my DNA to be popular.

SINEAD

A couple of years after school was over and I was working as a secretary at a piddly little job that I had zero to no interest in, when Catriona, a friend from school called me. Catriona had been Sinead's pal and had been mine for a while in school but I wasn't her number one choice for palling around. I knew this and it rarely bothered me. I was just happy to be liked in some manner and accepted. Catriona said Sinead was home from her travels and needed a friend to hang out with.

Most of our year had emigrated, or God forbid, gotten married or pregnant. It was a toss-up. Instantly I said yes, yes, yes, yes! There are moments when you know your life is turning, towards what isn't so clear, but its turning, and turning means moving, and moving feels good. So I met Sinead the next night and we were inseparable for six glorious months of mischief.

Mam loved Sinead too. She made herself at home instantly. She was easy to love but wild at heart and maybe she herself knew it. Maybe she knew there was little time, so we could forgo sleep and thrive on late nights, a bit of boozing and silly boys. She was right on – we could and we did until one day when the wet Dublin streets and a big green bus took her away. No warning. Bye-bye. I became crippled by the unsaid and unlived.

At nineteen years old, I didn't know what to do with death, where to put it. So I put it away, filed it with all the other parts of life I couldn't understand or comprehend deep into my soggy Irish heart, which was lost in the fog of grief that I did well to cover up for many, many years.

Life went on and I moved to America, and on trips home I could not help but think of her and our glory days. We were renowned by folks for our pub antics and stories. We never failed to put a smile on her Dad's face or my Mam's. We wormed our way into people's hearts without really trying. So it was easy to come home and find people and reminisce about times gone by. And it was during two of these trips that Sinead had her way of letting me know she was still very much around.

Aisling and Richella were Sinead's sisters. They lost their older sister too, just like I'd lost my best friend. But I left Ireland and they remained, coping with the loss as best they could. Now Dublin is not a small city. So bumping into people can happen, but rarely.

One night when I had come home for a visit, my family took me outside of Dublin to another county for dinner, miles away from the city itself. Coming home, I always felt Sinead's spirit, or at least I would be reminded of her more often through the smells of Dublin, which took me back in time, especially the noise of pubs and restaurants. So being in a busy restaurant was quite the setting to be reminded of her and good times. Irish people know how to get together and create a buzz. We love life and social settings and the art of conversation is something that is nicely embedded into our Celtic fiber along with a fancy for a jar or two. Either way, we make the most of things and rarely complain or is that just my fanciful memory?

Sitting at the table, I looked around at the chatting faces of customers, happy with their evening, having fun only to stop on a face I slightly recognized. I began to scan the internal portfolio of faces in my head, the way one does when they see somebody they haven't seen in a while. Only I had to flick through it a few more times until I found myself standing up and walking over to the table, awash in the moment with a slow motion of memory. A gentle spirit was nudging me closer, saying *don't stop, keep moving.* Then as I stood at the table beside the girl sitting down, she tilted her head up towards me racing through her own portfolio and as time stood still, we both recognized each other. Our hearts connected, our eyes the same. Aisling, Sinead's sister stood and we hugged each other to death.

As we sat outside the restaurant in the dark, damp Irish, night we chatted on for what seemed like hours, still amazed at the synchronicity of it all, knowing this was orchestrated by Sinead and no other. You see, Aisling had no intention of going out that night. Not until her neighbors a few houses down knocked on her door and insisted she come out for dinner. She wasn't in the mood, even slightly, but they would not leave her alone. So begrudgingly, she threw on a jacket and came out – and there I was. It was the most memorable of nights as we recounted old times and told stories of Sinead and the past. It was a golden memory and still is.

A few years went by and we lost touch. Actually we didn't keep in touch and that was ok. We felt so healed from the night and comforted by it that we allowed it be what it was. But that wasn't to be the end of it. People do maintain their traits, even on the other side and Sinead was no exception. She never took no for an answer.

On another trip home, sitting in a little pub, watching the world walk by in Dublin City, a dark haired woman walked by and in an instant I rapped on the window, trying to catch her attention. Aisling, I yelled, Aisling! Again we sat in the pub giddy with delight at the sequence of events that wrapped us in a warm glow that time would never, ever erase. Sinead was as busy in spirit, connecting those she loved together.

Myself and Aisling have remained in touch throughout the years. Since that last encounter, we have gone back and forth over the Atlantic to see each other for fun. And other times, I've been transported across the ocean by the lightning bolt of death, ushered back to the water's edge of my birthplace for goodbyes gone bad-byes.

At my Mam's funeral mass, I sat in the front row as is customary for the family, my head down as people came up to get communion, my tears hitting the pew. I was dying for it all to be over when I felt a soft hand gently pat me on the head. I looked up and there was Aisling – but the touch, the touch wasn't her. I don't know how I knew this but that inner voice told me this was not what it appeared to be. Aisling looked at me as if to say she could feel it too. Embarrassed, she continued back to her seat until the mass was over.

After the mass, I met Aisling outside where she apologized for touching my head because you just don't do that. She said as she walked by me with my head down, her heart went out to me and before she could stop it her hand was on my head – but she said she felt it wasn't her hand at all. "Lizzy," she said, "I think that was Sinead because I would never have done that."

I agreed. It felt angelic and knowing, full of love and history. We both knew what was at the heart of it and we were not to be persuaded otherwise. We hugged each other tightly, pretending nothing, believing everything.

Sinead was my best friend. She spoiled me for all other friendships and to date, I've never quite bonded with another. I don't know if my heart could take another *best friend loss* and to be honest, I don't think connections like that come around twice in a lifetime. It was the pure definition of 'friendship' and I'm quite confident that if I looked up the word friendship in the dictionary, it would have her face beside it.

Oh, and on Aisling's recent trip here to San Diego, we drove to Palm Springs to spend a glorious girlie weekend in the sun at a lovely posh hotel and upon checking in, the lady asked Aisling where she was from. She said "Dublin".

The lady was shocked and said, "You came all that way?"

We thought, hey, let's see where this goes and we said, "Why yes, yes of course we did."

Immediately she took our key and handed us a different one, smiled and went back to her work. Upon entering the room we just dropped our bags. We had been upgraded to a suite that sat on some gorgeous grounds, with chairs dangling from the ceiling, four poster beds, a balcony fit for royalty and we knew that Ireland had nothing to do with it whatsoever.

Water to Tears

I've thought of you
Of what I might give you
Of what you don't already have
Is it my heart?
Is it my heart?
Is it my heart?
What could I bring you
that you don't already have?
Like trees to a forest
Gold to the sun
White to snow
Water to tears
I'd bestow upon you
Something just because
It's what we have come to expect
But I shan't
No need
Don't stir
Exhale the longing
You have what matters most
You've had it long before we met
Many moons ago in exchange
For another time
The only thing worth giving
The only thing there is
My love

Elibrown
San Diego Strand

Elibrown was my second cat. He was easy to love. Ginger tabby boys are quite distinctly the best. He loved to pounce on Fiona and pull out great wads of her white hair, much to her annoyance. He was however, for the most part (Fiona might disagree), extremely lovable and just an all around good boy, trying his best to purr me away from disaster. He worked his way into my heart easily and there he stayed for fourteen years. He came to no harm.

A month or so after my Dad died, Elibrown got a limp that I did nothing about. I thought the little guy had just fallen and hurt himself and, to be honest, I felt like abused elastic in a fat lady's knickers – barely holding on – in no shape to care beyond the moment. I was in a semi-kind-of-grief and my idea at that point of a crises had been tipped in a titanic direction of calamities.

Thanksgiving was upon us and that morning Eli couldn't jump up to get his food on the counter where it always sat. I felt a familiar twinge in my heart telling me this was more than a sprain but I had no place to put the feeling, so I filed it away. He looked at me trying his best to hide his own fear and worry so I would be ok.

A day later his paw began to swell and still I did nothing. I was useless with fear. I still hoped this would go away. Irish to the core. It didn't. A couple of days later Elibrown has an episode on my bed, a turn, and after an emergency visit to the vet we knew our time together was in short supply. His little furry heart had run out of tick-tocks. Wrapped in a second-hand fraying towel, we went home to unravel together.

After battling cancer with Fiona, losing my Mum to cancer a few months after and then my Dad a month prior to this, I was strangely ok with taking him home and doing our best until the end. At that point I had no fight left in me and hoped to God Eli knew more than I did.

I am blessed to have an amazing friend who is a holistic veterinarian and together we decided homeopathy and palliative care would do the job. Three days later while I was giving Elibrown tender kisses, his pulse slowing down I said, "Listen Eli, I'm going to watch a bit of telly. You stay here love and call out if you need me."

I had just walked into the other room when he cried out, the loudest cry I ever heard from him and I ran back to his bedside, popped his *gotta-go-now* body into my arms and watched his flame of life go out. He stretched out his arms, said "Excuse me, I gotta go," and exhaled for the very last time and made his transition, peacefully.

I know it may not sound right to some, but it was beautiful. Eli did show me the way, every step he told me what he wanted, who he wanted to see and how much he could be touched and caressed. I read his signs perfectly. I honored his life fully and buried him under a tree – the Eli tree and there he rests today, back to the musky ground.

Three days later, reeling from the loss, I lay down on my healer's table, left alone with some acupuncture. Enveloped in lovely music and wrapped in a warm blanket, a wave of drenching sadness washed over me. I hadn't expected it, but there it was followed by a familiar feeling upon my chest, little paws making cookies. It was my Eli, come back to do some healing, massaging my heart like he loved to do, trying even in spirit to take away my pain. All I could feel was love, undiluted and simple, the same kind of love I felt for everyone I have ever loved and lost. He had come to no harm.

After my session, I went for a walk on the beach which has cleansing abilities way beyond anything else I have known in this lifetime. It's magical that way. And as I walked along the shimmering shore, remembering all those who had passed on, I turned and out of the corner of my eye I saw him. Mr. Elibrown walking away in the same direction my Mam went that day on the beach – not so long ago. He turned back and gave me one last glance, and then trotted off.

Bye, bye Elibrown, you have been loved.

Believe

There are so many reasons to not
And only one to believe

Each day delivers a different blow
to the candle of ego

There are many ways
But only one solution
to unbanjax this heart

It floats in and out
Embarking upon laws against regret
And the sweet breath of a fragile life
Lands itself upon my neck
Drying salty tears away
away

While the candle burns
beyond the flame
into the forgotten pieces
of this beautiful life

Dad
Major Tom

My Dad, Tommy Allen went fast. Three days in the hospital. Three daughters by his bedside, knowing the man we called our Dad, was getting ready to leave.

Tom put up a good fight, so to speak, which was in keeping with his spirit. He was a fighter, yet I didn't know my Dad that well. He rarely shared much of himself with us. He had more of a love affair with the drink, yet I know he loved us in his own way. But he hadn't always been an easy man to love, but that's for a different book entirely.

My sister Christine was the one on the final watch. Myself and Louise had gone back to her house outside of Dublin for a nap and a shower. We would be back, we promised, in the morning. Christine, exhausted from the flight from San Diego made a bed on the floor of the cold tiled room that would have made a Saint shiver, yet she said she'd be grand and she was for a while. But at four-twenty that next morning, our Dad slipped away, with Christine by his side. Myself and Louise dashed to the hospital but he was nowhere to be found.

After the body was taken down into the bowels of the hospital underground, all three of us made our way back to Louise's house which sits on one of the most gorgeous golf courses in Ireland. It's just the best place you would want to be, especially in the aftermath of loss. Golf courses are spiritual places and I didn't have to play golf to know that. But Dad did. He had been an avid golfer all his life; he knew their healing properties. So it was fitting we all went back there together.

I took a walk outside the restaurant as my sisters ordered some breakfast, just for something to do. There would be no stopping this day. The morning was coming in, the fog gently rolling away as I felt a soft hand on my face, a slight brush against my skin. For a moment, I couldn't catch my breath. I may have stopped breathing altogether, but it was a feeling-touch of knowing which left me most assured it was my Dad's spirit – taking flight across the golf course, his most favorite place. And in an instant, it was gone, leaving me alone once again as the fog carried my Dad onwards to his destination. He was finally free. And I thought to myself how long this man had waited for this feeling.

The day of the funeral came and we drove in the silence that funerals warrant towards the church, all of us in one car, bundled up like Irish penguins, watching Dublin City smear past us. The driver had the radio on which we were grateful for as it canceled out any need for conversation – though I couldn't tell you what was playing until it came on. I turned to my sisters and squeezed their hands, tears filling our eyes, listening to David Bowie singing Space Oddity.

That day us girls were in no doubt at all that our Dad was coming through to us, just days after he passed, sending his love to us, letting us know he had touched down, so to speak.

D A D

Spirit will come in any door it can and my Dad didn't even have to knock that loudly. Just soft and gentle, like peace.

The Turn

Today my Dad had a turn
He kept on turning
I ran to his side
Helped him to his bed
Wrapped my arms around him and
Prayed

I prayed for everything all at once
Life, death and everything in between
I prayed that I would know what to do
That I could do something
That he would let me

His breath quickened
His words slurred
I asked him what he wanted
He didn't know
I didn't know either

We both sat there in not knowing
I am Familiar with that place
I think he knows it too
I helped him lie down when he could
And rubbed his back as he lay Catching his breath
Any breath

Me catching tears as they formed and pushing them back
As they Swarmed like bees inside
Stinging my insides out

D A D

His crinkled body lay shattered and skinny
Going back to the shape of Childhood
My hands trying to bring a kind of comfort
I didn't know I had

I wondered if this was THE END
For him and for me
If we could both just slip away together
Silently
Simply

He began to mutter about old age and how awful it was
How bushed he felt
And why it wasn't possible to just vanish when we were done
How the body fails us big-time
How hard it must be to live with bricks for feet and
A sponge for a heart

He talked of things like euthanasia and Amsterdam
We laughed instead of crying
He began to shudder back to life
Saying Saturday morning was no time to solve the world's
problems
Brushing off the sentiment like excess talc off a baby's bum
Or suchlike

And we got him up and dressed
And down the stairs
Before Mam came home from town
Before it would ruin her day

I winked at him
Looking and feeling paper thin
Flat and pale
My wasting away kept inside
And With the kettle on

Another day
Thankfully
Boiled to life

~ Dad,
At what point did you know
I loved you? ~

Dad Again
Buck Up

Ok. I have to preface this story and say this one is absolutely fab. Dad scored big time and I am sure he knows it. A powerful man and dare I say it Dad, you're a bit more creative on the other side than you ever were here. Just saying.

So about a year after my Dad had passed I hadn't really mourned his loss too much. I don't think I had too much to mourn. We hadn't been too close and he hadn't made such an impact on my life. Well he did, but more so by his absence rather than his presence.

I believe we are here to learn some lessons. Life's a school and it would be amiss of us to not hit the ground running and do what we can in the time that we have. And I don't think anyone here is having too much of a different experience than the next person. Really. Forgiveness, unconditional love, respect, compassion, acceptance and that most elusive one – finding peace. Yes, there are many variances of those themes for each person but we are more often having a common experience than a unique experience. At least that has been my take so far, and I'm ok with that. What it means for me is that I might have more in common with people than I ever imagined and this helps me not feel so isolated, and that is most definitely a good thing.

So back to Dad. Growing up, Dad wasn't the paternal type. He'd appear at intervals and throw us a smile, a joke, maybe even some candy when we were sick and a quick check in to see how we were doing. Mam really ran the house. But when we were out of sorts at times or sad, he knew this but he had no way of reaching out to us. He just hadn't learned it or seen much tenderness in his own childhood, so it was not something he could easily and readily relate to. In fact, he never said out loud that he loved me until the day I got married. A bloody long time. I still get a strange feeling in my belly remembering those words in my ear as we did the Father-Daughter dance.

"Lizzy, you know I love you, don't you?"

"Yes Dad, yes I do."

"Good," he said. "Good."

And I was like, this was supposed to be my day, Dad. Every other one was yours.

An entire childhood rushed at me with the force of a raging bull and I did my best to hold it back. The air around me swelled nonsense, big things to say, but I let them fall around my newly-wed feet, like excess confetti and danced over them. Our lives were swollen with the unsaid and I knew all it would take would be one tiny prick and the past would burst forth upon us all like a tsunami. So today only the little things would get said. Little things holding many secrets.

At times, and again this is quite the Irish saying, so not too unique to my Dad but for the story, it's relevant; people use the term buck-up. It is exactly as it sounds. Say it out loud to yourself. You've really very little choice except to perk-up or buck-up. It's meant to get you out of yourself in a fun way. Stop taking yourself so seriously is how I understand and feel it. Life's good. Move on. Get on with living. And that was my Dad. He tried his best to make the most of things, when he could. He was happy with the simple things and he was kind. He was that.

So about a year after he had passed, I was having a moment. I have many of them, but this one was on a wet, rainy day. I was missing him, wanting to give him a call, allowing the wet weather to have its way with me, bringing me back to my gray childhood and Ireland. And as I was walking back to my car I glanced at a white car parked close by and saw a license plate: "BuckUp." Instantly I knew Dad was sending me a sign, one that needed no translation, no medium, no tarot cards, no meditation, nothing. It was plain and simple. It was my Daddy.

The rest of the day I experienced a quiet euphoria in my heart. I felt so connected not just to him, but to myself, to that inner knowing, to God, to source, to everything that has an ounce of energy of love. Time stood still. Time was obliterated. Time didn't matter. What mattered was how I felt and how the longing for my Dad now seemed silly because I felt him deep inside me. There, always there. Living just has a way of making us forget.

Last week, a year on, I could feel my grip on sanity loosening again. It's funny the things that will undo us. I thought I had it together. I was feeling so in alignment with source, nature, what have you. Then I got a bad haircut. It simply ruined me. Listen, I've had some appalling haircuts. Catastrophic. And I've not been blessed with much of it. Nope. My sisters got that gene pool. God saw fit to give me a fast metabolism and a sparkling wit. He is fair after all. But with so many tragic haircuts under my skinny belt, another one was just too much for me to handle. So I crumbled into an abyss of self-pity and anguish. I couldn't fathom why I kept having this life-lesson. I couldn't even glance in a mirror. I felt ugly and unlovable. So being inclined to sadness, I fell right into the well of self-pity missing everyone: Dad, Mam, my animals, my youth, Ireland, my sisters, youth (again), good TV and everything in between. I was in a fetal position for a day. I cried myself into the night, asking my parents for a sign to let me know I wasn't alone, cursing God for not answering me either. Why in the world am I here, what is my purpose, why so much pain? And on, and on until I fell into the arms of some kind of drenched, exhausted, pathetic sleep.

The next morning on the way to work I was coming out of the fog, my hair a mix of product and anger, the sunny day reflecting strongly against my intolerance of all things light, but I knew I was going to be ok. As I drove down the main highway of the town where I work, I thought of my Dad as a hawk flew overhead. I believe his spirit lives on in them and as a white car drove past me on my left, I glanced at it, once again reading the license plate, "BuckUp." Same white car, God bless it. I wonder who drives it. I wonder if I will ever see it again.

These days no matter where I am or how I feel, I know my Dad is close. He's a breath away, looking over me now, so much more capable in spirit to do so. He's the same over there too. Probably cracking some highly inappropriate jokes with the angels, driving my Mam mad. He's kept his sense of humor for sure and he won't be denied the additional joy of reaching out to his daughter in her time of need, and letting her know that she is loved, never alone, and that there is nowhere her name cannot be heard.

TD's Tears

The Irish night tucks us in just fine
beside me
He utters what seems like nonsense
says he wants to take Lizzy home
yet here I sit creased beside him
I'd go you know
I'd go in his place
but instead he makes plans
with his Lord
his God
he knows
he definitely knows
that the tick is being taken
out of tock

Nana
Scent of Memory

My Nana was the nucleus of our family and when she passed my Mam seemed to take on that role, at least as a child that is what I felt over the years. My Nana was the nuts and bolts of our family and as children we gravitated to her with the magnetic force of a million friendly planets. And when she passed, she left a Nana-sized-whole in our little universe.

Nana had boobs, boobs she passed down to my sisters but once again not me. Nope, I missed the boob train – fast metabolism and all that shite, remember? Nevertheless, as a kid I would run towards her and get nestled in them and I would feel so safe, like a swimmer might as they swim towards a continental shelf in a warm ocean. It felt like home, wrapped in her Nana mixture of baked goods, old perfume and a mischievous smile. Evelyn O'Hagan, God how I loved her. How she knew me. How she made me feel loved and not so strange. She used to bounce me up and down on her knees as she listened to Neil Diamond records, smoking her cigars. *Sweet Caroline* is all I have to hear and I am there in that old house, wrapped in her mahogany love.

At fifteen I was too young to process her death, even as I saw her in the morgue all done up like, and with a look on her face which said cancer hadn't won. It really hadn't been a battle at all. She was the one who looked victorious. Even in death, she possessed a grace few could dream of having while alive. Either way, she'd gone off to rest after a much-lived-life. But I wasn't too sad then and I'm not now. It was my Mam I was worried about. Always.

Many years on, having moved away and gotten on with my life, my sister Louise had a child Max, a gorgeous little boy and I wanted to know if my Nana was around. I was curious if she was looking over the first grandchild in the family. Even though I had gone home to see my sister for the couple of weeks after Max arrived, I felt I needed to know Nana was around. It was a quiet prayer I prayed, not giving it much heed, but for some reason I couldn't let it go. It might also be worth noting that when I found out she named him Max I was troubled because my heart told me his name was supposed to be Luke. I never told her that as it seemed so strange. Max, I said, but his name is Luke, Luke Cunningham. Still Max it was, and is.

One evening around that time, I arrived home, walked in the door and felt the need to just sit on the couch in the darkness. I lived in an old house, which I think bodes well for spirits to make their visits. I just do. It's another one of my many beliefs. So when I sat down and closed my eyes, a smell I can easily describe as my Nana's kitchen, wafted up my nose like an old friend. *Hello, remember me?*

Right away I was brought back to her tiny kitchen in that big house. It was unmistakable. She *was* here and as soon as it came, it was gone and I sat there alone, covered in goose bumps (the good kind) and comfort. She'd let me know she was around and could see everything. But that wasn't all.

A couple of weeks later, the same thing happened. I walked in, sat on the couch and didn't close my eyes this time. I felt a chill come over me and out of the corner of my eye, to the left, a white figure appeared. It was my Nana, of that I was so sure, but again as soon as it registered with me, and I fully looked in that direction, she was gone. The moment lingered as I could feel her softly leave me be. She did what I asked her to do and even more than I ever imagined.

I don't think I ever told Louise about it. I didn't need to tell anyone. I believe it was just for me. I knew from that moment on, Nana was watching over Max and Louise and was enjoying the experience of being a Great Grandmother, even from the other side. And today my sister Louise has two lovely boys, Max and Benn Luca.

No Returning

I feel her at times
wanting to melt
into the invisible space
where she has never quite made it to
Because she knows if she dares
There will be no returning

And I plant a kiss where only a kiss can be felt
On a furrowed angel's brow
Her oak eyes closing under the heavy curtain of the day
Exhaling a responsible breath
Between the ticking of Motherhood
A sometimes chosen life

But in a rare moment
When she drapes herself just so
Exhaling the day around her
Chiffon with tenderness
That falls like lemon gold to my freckled skin
Sanding my sharp edges
Tasting like gold
I feel there will be no returning

~ If I travel the length and breath
of love
Will I find you again? ~

Dexter

Life Brushes By

S ome dogs just have quite the magnificent, predestined life and Dexter was one of those lucky dogs. He knew why he was here and what he was here to do. He found Tori easily, bounded out of the shelter, black as soot and into her heart, and there he stayed for seventeen sweet years.

Tori loved him so much that when she opened her healthy pet store she named it after him – Dexter's Deli. Talk about a mission! Together they set out to teach people how to feed their pets real food and get serious about their animal's health, whether they wanted to know it or not. They were not here to sugar-coat the truth on any level and Dexter was a living testament to their life's purpose.

Dexter was the ultimate picture of canine health – and dedicated to Tori and not in a typical "dog" way. It went beyond that. This was a soul contract. Nobody else was even mildly interesting to him. He had the hook-up and every other dog knew it. He had a blessed life with more social engagements than most people; more parties, celebrations and life experiences, but as is the case with all of God's creatures, social or not, their lives too must come to an end.

On a November day, Dexter took a turn from which there would be no turning back. He had a seizure which took away most of his much-loved freedom. Tori knew their time together was in short supply, as she set about organizing her life so she could spend whatever time was left with him.

Most people she knew could not understand why she wouldn't put Dexter to sleep considering his limited capabilities at that point. Those who thought that just didn't understand Tori and Dexter's unique bond, and nobody outside of the pair of them needed to.

During the gift of Dexter's final weeks, Tori embraced the task ahead and spent it nestled up with him at home, tending to his every need. This she needed more than air and the legacy she wanted him to leave would be one of a majestic departure matching his majestic life.

For a couple of weeks she was at his beck and call, helping him do everything he could not do for himself and every once in a while, she would get a flicker of the old Dexter back, enough to help her carry on with his palliative care, which of course included the odd slice of crispy bacon and a bit of chocolate. He was doing just fine. They both were. In a world where we are programmed to hasten a "painful experience" to its conclusion, there seemed nothing critical about it all. They would finish this journey together just like they lived it, in Dexter time.

I kept my distance. This is what I hoped for. I urged her to stay home, to take him out for a drive, to the beach, anywhere. She joked that people thought she was going mad, carrying her dying dog everywhere with her. But she quickly figured out she didn't care what others thought, as she sat on the beach at sunset, Dexter wrapped up nice and tight, saying goodbye to the blessing of another day.

I watched her tend to him and her heart break wide open with every episode. She reached for anything to make him feel better, whatever the moment demanded and whenever she thought he was ready to go, he'd rally. We both laughed and cried a lot, our hearts wrung out and dry from the possibility of hope.

Animals like to stay until they know, just like people, that we will be ok. They hang on with all their might until they are most sure, and even when you think you've told them a million times that it's ok to go, they seem to know if that is in actuality the truth or just rhetoric. They read the language of the heart perfectly. Dexter was no exception. But every passing night became more and more restless and the days so hard on them both. Tori knew she had to let him go and that they would probably need some help.

We were blessed to have a wonderful friend Tamara, who is a true-and-through holistic veterinarian. Not just slightly, but absolutely. Tamara honors the human-animal bond even in the face of possible head-scratching from others. She is like an animal herself. She doesn't care what people think. She knew of the bond between Dexter and Tori and had treated Dexter over the years, which wasn't often, because *that dog* was the epitome of health. But when asked to hold ceremony for Dexter's final moments, Tamara agreed with all the grace and kindness she is known to have.

So with myself and Tori's best friend Gale, Tamara, and a cold December night, we honored the passing of a magnificent being from this earth. Dexter was ready. He sat in Tori's arms, cushioned right into her lap, his eyes closed, already sleeping his way into the arms of angels. Within minutes he was gone, the room awash with soft music and tears.

It was as royal a moment as one could hope to experience. The passing of a much-lived-life. The grief was palpable as we all stood up to say our last goodbyes. It was obvious Dexter had departed, his body cooling already underneath the touch. How does one cope with the immediate departure of an animal? Where do we put our heart until we are ready to face life again?

I'd known Tori for some time. It was easy to see where Dexter got his grace from. On that night, I drove Tori down to the beach where Dexter loved to run and play so she could say one more goodbye. The night had turned to complete darkness and the weather had risen up to meet our emotions. As we walked onto the beach, the wind really started up. Strange how there is a special kind of wind reserved for lamenting on beaches. Personally, I believe it's imported from Ireland.

We walked out close to the shore, the wind crescendo-ing around us, feeling as though we would be whisked up and away, which wouldn't have been a bad thing considering. But as we stood hugging each other against the wind, sand whipping around us like the most abrasive of emotions, letting us know the weather had no intention of going anywhere except right there, something magical happened. The wind turned to the texture of love and departure, a navy meringue of momentum and mischief.

Dexter's spirit had not left yet. He was having one final goodbye as he wrapped himself around us, brushing up against Tori while planting a celestial dog kiss on her face. As he completed one final mad lap around our bodies, he darted like a young puppy right out into the ocean of forever and forget-me-not. And in the next instant we knew he had been whisked away, ready for his next big adventure.

As we walked back to the car, the wind almost gone, no words were necessary between us. They would have dismantled the moment and we wanted to savor it. We knew we had just experienced the passing of Dexter's spirit into the next world, where he would never stop running and chasing and darting in and out of adventure. The end of his life hadn't been anything to fear at all. The connection Tori had with him would span galaxies and lifetimes.

To this day we call December "Dextember" as Tori continues to celebrate Dexter's life through Dexter's Deli, a place where pet owners come with their animals for comfort and friendship, help, love and good food.

Dexter's final goodbye, his life brushing past us, came at just the right time. It didn't stop the grief Tori felt, or would feel in the coming weeks and months. She had to go through it like everyone else and just like Dexter, she did it with grace and a few tissues.

This story always reminds me of the power of an animal's love, to let us know their spirit rejoices in release from this physical plane, and that there is no doubt that as soon as they can, they will give us a sign that they are on their way home.

Vein of Gold

And in thine eyes a glimmer of hope
That resurrects the damp from these pale days
Mixing with the crushed powder of a previously saturated heart
Wrung out and dry from the possibilities of hope
The destitution of despair
And as too does a rosebud in winter
Dream of spring bloom
We fall limp at the feet of what we cannot change
The seasons of love, of hurt, of pain, of joy
Move through us like wind through barley
Allowing the noise of life abound
And you say you want to fly
Fly away with me
But why would you
When I will never leave
But remain forever in your heart
As a vein of gold

*~ Everything brings
enlightenment
There is no way to get it wrong ~*

Five Sisters
After All These Years

As a kid, I used to do a bit of babysitting, though it was rarely for babies, as the title implies. It was for a bunch of sisters in our estate, five to be exact. Yes, five of them all ranging from the age of twelve down to yuck, six months. The Mum had gotten remarried after the girls Dad passed and produced a boy. Now, I was at a bit of a loss on how to take care of him, but thankfully the oldest girl had that covered and I just entertained the others; aka, watched telly with them and ate them out of house and home. There was nobody better suited for this low-paying, high-caloric job. It was a much-needed break for a teenage girl from a full house of her own.

I loved my nights munchin' my way through all the food groups that never seemed to appear in our house; crisps, chocolate, pastas, sandwiches. I would roll out of there five pounds heavier, leaving no crumb behind. It was always something I enjoyed immensely but there was a sad feeling to it, a feeling that seemed to lay on the house in a sticky film kind of way. Mystery and loss maybe or shades of something in-between. The girls Dad had shot himself in the bathroom a few years prior and really who recovers from that?

For a bunch of girls, there was very little mischief. They seemed to be preoccupied with other things and yet polite. I am sure their hearts were confused. As the story goes, their Dad had gotten himself into quite a financial bind and just could not recover. I don't even think his wife knew how bad it was. Maybe five kids had something to do with that, but whatever the case he didn't share it with her and the pressure got to be too much. One evening he told her to take them all out to the shops and get them something nice and off they went only to return to a locked bathroom. Upon opening they found their Dad had shot himself. I can't imagine what ensued. Suffice to say there's no recovering from such a thing, none at all but life did go on and there I was in the house itself.

There was a clock on the mantle that had been stopped the day he died. It sat there, quiet as a clock can be but still strange to me because a clock's job and its only job is to tell the time. It was jobless, unemployed, laid-off. It troubled me – that and the smell. The house maintained an "odor-identity" I could not name. Maybe it was cooking mixed with sadness but it wasn't anything I remember smelling before and after. It was exclusive to the sisters' house. I'd go searching for the origin of it some nights, only to find nothing.

Years on, and I'm back home for a visit, and I see one of the daughters, older now, walking down our street and I ask my Mam, "Is that one of the sisters?"

"Why yes, yes it is."

She looked sad to me like one gentle touch would spill a mile of hurt. And I thought of what kind of life she had. I wondered if she found some peace with it all and if her sisters had also. At that particular moment, I was grateful for my life and that was indeed and of itself a rare moment, so I seized it and gave my Mum a hug, the big round the waist Mother hugs. Nothing like it.

Fast forward to my house in San Diego, during the time my Nana had come to visit me to let me know she was still around looking over us all, enjoying being a part of our life even on the other side. I had a moment that I recalled being significant. It happened in that old house again.

One evening I was sitting on that thought-provoking couch, quiet, reading, as another smell wafted into the room. It was still, asking for permission to enter but then not waiting for a response. It engulfed a sense I can only describe as a sixth one, because it was all of them plus one, the one that deciphers what cannot be physically measured. The lay-a-way sense. It was the five sisters' house. It was their Dad. Maybe he had noticed I was doing a bit of a service for others and spirits are funny, they'll try to barge their way in given the slightest opportunity. They're not in the habit of waiting for a written invitation.

I wondered what he wanted me to do and then I sort of felt he wanted me to pass on a message to his daughters, to let them know he was ok and that he was still looking over them. How in God's name could I do that all the way in America? Well, truth was, I couldn't. I didn't want to. What would I say? "Hey, yer Da wants to say hello. Do you remember me?" I'd be certified as nuts and carried off to the loony bin. They have those in Ireland. So I didn't do anything, in fact I got a bit scared. I didn't know how it could happen if I hadn't asked for it. I can only assume from other experiences to date that if you have a gift, even if you don't package it for society, you still have it. And spirits, particularly those who might want to get a message to loved ones, spirits that might be trapped between two worlds, will grab onto the only person they think can to do the job for them.

I wonder over the years if I should have gone up to their house and knocked on the door but I can only assume that their Dad has found other ways to let them know he's ok and that he's sorry, because that is what I truly felt. I hope they have gotten over such a tragic loss and that their lives are full and they might have families of their own now and that they too know that their Dad is only a breath away.

The Heel of Plenty

Let the spider spin the web
Allow the sun to show the dirt
Feel the prism of joy that eclipses the dark
In the ocean inside

If pleasure is the absence of pain
How will we know?
Pleasure no longer buried
Permitted to bulge at the seams of a much-lived-life
Recognizable in every form by the soul's eye
Intertwined within that immeasurable distance between
the soul and the heart -
This is how

In grateful need of nothing I can do without
And grateful to those who share their reflections with me
In any and every form
I am blessed
It is plain to see
In my joyous breath
In my life's intent
Surfing on the heel of plenty

~ After the storm
I awoke in sawdust and sand
And I knew instantly
That it was all mine ~

God Himself
Póg Mo Thóin

The stories in this book are true accounts. I haven't even embellished them, which is part of my Irish heritage, but for this book – there was no need. They are in no need of fabrication and this story is no exception. It was during a time of deep introspection in my life, a time when I had to make a decision between living half or living whole.

I like my drink. I've always liked my drink. I think my Dad passed this down to me. I never got to thank him for that one but regardless, there came a time when drink stopped being my friend. It literally stopped liking me long before I stopped liking it. Close to the end of our love affair, I came across these words somewhere, which traveled deep into my soul. The exact words were *alcohol is the final battle*. The words gutted me, hitting a cord I didn't know I had, at the same time having no doubt it was meant for me. If I was to become, truly become, the person I knew I was destined to be, the person I could feel in my soul the world needed me to be, the person I could love without doubt or regrets, I'd have to give up my red wine – forever.

Easy enough. Not so much. It was going to put up a fight, and fight it did. It left me pulverized from an innocent night, whereupon I awoke and knew God had opened a window but that the window would close and it would not open again in my lifetime. I could feel the soft pulse of death beneath my skin, sticky and black. So I tried, I tried to go it alone. I failed. So I got help. It worked but not without work itself. I went at sobriety like a job. I wasn't going to fail and I wasn't going to die. For want of a better word, I got sober and the course it took, changed me from the inside out.

When everything is stripped away and you are left with yourself, just you – the meaning of life meanders a bit. During the days before my final solo attempt, I went to Idyllwild, a beautiful hamlet in the mountains North of San Diego, with my partner. I'd dragged her through the mess too. Yet I was loved beyond the word right into its very meaning. But we both knew a shift was coming. But still I held onto a bombastic thought that I would be ok if I could just manage a beer here or a glass of wine there. I'd literally become allergic to alcohol, and now, almost to myself. I was in a constant state of spiritual pain, which left me quite aware of the simple fact that there was no place to hide anymore, not even in Idyllwild.

Snow had fallen and had started a bit of a melt. The mountain was like the arm of a schoolgirl busy eating a melting ice cream on a warm Summer day. We went for hikes and lolled around in the cabin with the dogs, acutely aware that something was ending but not knowing exactly what that would be or even look like. We talked little that weekend. All the talking had been done. I half-heartedly drank a beer or two, not even wanting them. The unsaid carries more weight I've come to understand. And it was thick around us during that time, thick and heavy, wafting in and out of our almost conversations, like a resurfacing debt that would not be paid off by the usual methods.

The last morning in Idyllwild, I laced up for a run and headed off way up into the mountain, not caring if I'd ever come back. So I wasn't keen on looking at where I was going or any landmarks along the way. I'd run my way through my adult life. It's where I would meet God, out on those streets, smelling like sweat and tears, hard work and victory. He never failed to show up in all of his many disguises. So run I did, up the hills and down them, back up and down again, lost in a symphony of pain and sweat.

I cried as I ran. I let years of pain and loss find their way down my cheeks and nestle right into my neck, where they met up with all the other dried tears which had passed before them. It was a salty reunion of the old and the new. I cried for my Mum, my Dad, my animals, and everyone I had ever said goodbye to. I didn't care what I looked like. My soul dug deep into its socket and a scream escaped the deepest parts of myself that I had tucked away for far too long.

God please help me, help me feel good again, help me feel whole. Lift me up, take me away, do something. This life is killing me. It's too hard. I want to find peace and I don't know where it lives anymore, I don't think I ever did. I want to like myself, God. I want to be happy. Please, please don't leave me now when I need you most. Why do I feel so alone? Please, please give me a sign that you hear me. I need you now, not later, now!

I continued to run even though I had no idea where I was going. The sun was breaking through and hitting bits of snow, twinkling the day into sight. As I turned to go down a hill, which I can only assume led somewhere I hadn't been, I saw a car parked in the driveway of a beautiful, snow covered cabin. I stopped dead in my tracks. The license plate read "Póg mo Thóin" which translated means "Kiss My Arse." Now, I know God has a sense of humor. I'm well aware of that, but this time he found gold. This was his trump card and he knew when to play it. My Irish God had found his way to me all the way out here in Idyllwild. He had never left me after all.

I started to smile, then laugh to myself, then out loud. Absolutely perfect! This was my sign and only mine. It came in answer to my request. It came to let me know he was the one carrying me, he was there and I did indeed need to kiss his arse in order to live the life I was here to live. I needed to face my final battle knowing I would not be alone. I would be helped every step if I could just get out of the way and let him in and in the process stop taking myself so bloody seriously.

I was exhausted trying to justify my existence and hide my pain all these years. And as I wiped the final tears out of my eyes, getting ready for the hill back to the cabin, I noticed an old truck parked on the street which to my utter amazement also read "Póg mo Thóin", only with different lettering. Just in case I didn't get the message once, because we Irish are a thick-headed lot, God saw fit to tell me twice.

"Elizabeth" he said. "You have come a long way from where you were born to here, don't stop now and don't you dare lose your sense of humor, for you will need it in the days to come."

It was then that I noticed a man sitting in the garden, worn baseball hat, z-z-top beard working on something and I asked him, "Do you mind if I take a picture of the license plates?"

"No problem" he said, "but do you know what they mean?"

"Absolutely! I'm Irish."

"Ah, so you're not offended then."

"Not in the least."

From that day on I could feel another shift, subtle yet complex, dare I say it, like a vintage wine. I knew my rough edges would soften with time. God, I prayed they would but again I had an innate knowing I would be ok. I had the message

I believed was just for me, in only the way I would understand.

A customized sign from *Himself* that required no interpretation.

And yes, time has done its job once again.

Kissing The Bones

Here I am and it is inevitable
I am forever kissing the bones
Where the rapture that swarms the day
Will fade slower than melancholy

I no longer rise up nor do I land
This gray space absorbs me
I neither dissolve in water nor heat
Only trip down the light fantastic
Stripping the thread from the vein
For in blood there remains the remembrance of pain
Nothing strings together much
Only pearls and beans
These words exhale in jumbled disarray
As I love – I assume – everything from a distance

Even though HE has appeared before
And before me
Wrapping me in gold
While promising to present myself as treasure
I never fully unwrap
Where lies the origin of ache?
This ice will never melt
As I push the day away
While gripping my inner light
I appear to push out the cosmic pain
But I am aware fully
There remains no punishment more sincere than our own

GOD HIMSELF

When have we listened with such intent to silence
The sound where all others melt?
The golden liquid light has spilled and spoiled around me
Softly doing as much as it can
As much as I allow it sedate this man-made-pain
For it is inevitable
I am forever kissing the bones

Herding Harleigh
A Deliberate Life

The stars, the moon; they have all packed up and disappeared and left me in the twilight of his memory. My *Little Man* is gone and nothing, nothing can bring him back. I know this. Yet here I sit in the shadow of his memory, awash in snot and tears wondering what keeps the door of the heart from shutting permanently against the storm of departure. And, in usual Elizabeth fashion, a kind of cathartic-keyboard-madness ensues.

After finishing the first draft of my book, and being surprisingly pleased with the result – yet forever polishing it as a writer does, my *Little Man* Harleigh passed away on a Thursday morning. I should not have been so pleased, I tell myself. If I had been disgruntled and dissatisfied with my work, which was the usual climate in my writing world, then maybe the book wouldn't have needed another story. But unseen forces are always at work, I tell myself. Other forces which decided Harleigh would become the unexpected final chapter in a book which had no intention of ever bearing his name.

Harleigh was only seven years old and I was ill-prepared. I don't even know if the words will come, but I have to do something. Because I think I will go mad if I don't. You see, I want to follow him and I can't. I've got another little one still here who needs me now more than ever. Meanwhile my heart is bursting with an ocean of sadness that will most likely obliterate anything which stands in its way. And I think to myself, through the tears and the insanity that rolls over me like silent thunder, that no human heart can sustain such damage. If there were a NEMA for the heart, they would cut their losses on this one and move on. For inside this banjaxed organ, there are the makings for a flood that will end all floods.

Harleigh was an impulsive purchase. One hundred and fifty dollars and there I was driving home with a little brown fluff-ball of joy tucked in my t-shirt. He was my coming-out-of-a-relationship purchase. He would fill the void quite nicely, I imagined. *What will I call you?* At that precise moment a Harley Davidson bike drove by and that was it. *I'll spell it differently just to annoy people, just to be a little bit more contrived than I already was. Yes, perfect!*

He snuggled into what would eventually become his nook of choice, between my left shoulder and chin, and a love story began as my heart moved into a locked and fixed position in my chest, as though this was the piece that had always been missing. Harleigh was the rogue piece of myself I'd lived my entire life without, and in this fast moving world, we had managed to find our way to each other. And as I cuddled in close to him that very first night, inhaling the scent of unconditional love, I knew I had been moving toward him my entire life.

As I write this story about Harleigh, I wait patiently for a sign from him. But I don't know that I'm going to get one, not like the ones I've shared in this book. Maybe it's the fact it has just been a few days since the angels swept him away. Maybe I am too close to the pain. Maybe I won't get a sign. I don't know. Maybe his absence is the message. Maybe I've got to look in places I've never considered he might already be. I doubt this *Little Man* is going to be predictable even now. Christ almighty, I'm going to break.

Harleigh wasn't easy. He was anything but. At a young age, after a pretty horrific surgery, he shrunk against the world he found terrifying. All I could do was watch him and assure him things would be ok. *Something is wrong with my dog.* Something went so terribly wrong and nobody could see it but me, let alone stop it.

Harleigh saw the world differently. Every trip outside the front door was like the first. Every rock, every bird, every tree, every blade of grass – they were like a unique first time experience. But after his surgery, after the fear found a home in his body, he wouldn't let me come too close. A collar or a harness was out of the question. I could completely forget walking him on a leash or walking him at all, despite my vain attempts at trying. Dog trainers, soft collars, multiple treats, positive this, beneficial that – nothing worked to pull him back from his safe world. So I moved around him as softly as I could, herding him in as closely as he would let me; herding Harleigh, that was to become my mission for the next seven years.

After that initial surgery, the one where they tried to take care of everything that was "wrong" with him in one visit, neuter, hernia, too many teeth – he stopped playing too. Nothing excited him except my presence, or food, or as was more the case than not – both. He never fetched a thing, ran after a ball, chased another dog or person or greeted people in a friendly normal fashion. He barked them right out the door, all eight pounds of him. This made for few visitors. He couldn't figure out the peeing issue either. He grew up on pee pads, so all rugs were fair game. I managed well with it, though at times I could have sent him off for a doggie castration. And as for poop, it scared him beyond all reason. He ran away from it as fast as his little legs could carry him. And God forbid if it got attached to his fuzzy behind, for he would let a cry out of him that would have neighbors thinking he was indeed getting that aforementioned castration.

I don't think he understood the process itself – moving as he pooped, always trying to be one little Chihuahua step ahead of it. Maybe that caused him pain also. Who knew? What I did know was that the *Little Man* knew what he could and couldn't tolerate, and there was zero room for compromise. So I let him be himself, no matter how strange he seemed to anyone else. Like a skinny branch on a windy day, tall and straight against the sky he defied explanation. He became his own essential self and I loved him even more for it. And for as much as it appeared that our physical world was shrinking, my internal world was shifting in ways I could never have imagined. I didn't know it at the time, but I was expanding so I could fit his absence.

As the years moved on, Harleigh moved into early arthritis at the age of five. His hip almost lost its grip on his little body and a fall off the bed brought us back to the surgeon's table once more. He never recovered from that one. He looked at me like I was responsible for the pain. "How could you, Mum," his watery chocolate eyes awash in confusion. "How could you? You promised no more pain." So I did after that. No more. We worked with the pain, tried a bit of swimming for a while although we stopped when it appeared he might come close to having a stroke, at least that was the very clear impression his face was having on us all. The instructor hadn't seen the likes of it before, so we cut our losses after a couple of sessions, shook the excess chlorine and relief off in unison and trudged on.

I wanted to find a purpose for Harleigh and I couldn't. He didn't care for other dogs, other people; exercise equaled pain, though he tolerated my monthly attempts at a trip to the park or the beach, which only served to produce more wonderment, with a dollop of stark reality – this was no ordinary dog. Maybe he wasn't a dog at all. What I did know for sure, Harleigh loved two things; food and me. I came to the exhausted conclusion after many dollars and fruitless attempts at massage, acupuncture, aromatherapy, laser therapy, chiropractic and beyond – that it had to be enough. He seemed rather fine with it. Maybe if I'd stopped for a moment and softened into the experience, I would have found out earlier that I was Harleigh's purpose. I was his reason for being.

Harleigh followed me everywhere, always at my feet. I called it the "Harleigh dance" because you had to move with it. A few times he got stepped on, but rarely because when love runs around the rooms with you, you really don't mind dancing with it. We moved with grace and ease around each other. All this time though, Juno, my other love bug, was left a bit in the shadows. His health wasn't so much my priority at times. He seemed to be doing well. His dental could wait. He was content and enjoying life.

In December, Juno went in for his dental cleaning and came away without seventeen of his little teeth and with one rotten diagnosis of heart disease. How was I going to manage? Where would my life expand to fit the ever-growing number of veterinary appointments? My funds were quickly evaporating and my anxiety and sleepless nights increased. My own heart was having trouble keeping a safe beat. What was a safe beat anyhow? Who had one, and where for the love of God could I buy it?

On good days, days when Harleigh would let a most wonderful lady adjust him, which was rare, he slept all the way home. And I'd think to myself, *this hour drive and half a day is worth it. Look at him. He's doing great!* I came to another conclusion – he did it for me. He cooperated because I felt better. Yet, I knew it took all he had to not want to tear the head off anybody who attempted to touch him, even with medication, flower essences, homeopathy or anything else I could get my hands on. Harleigh was not in the business of trusting anybody. Full bloody stop!

And so it went. About a month ago, Harleigh had a turn. I thought it was his patella giving him trouble. It had been dislocated for some time now but I was doing my best to keep him comfortable. But when this episode happened, he stiffened up and keeled over. It looked like he might be having a stroke. Yet I'd never seen one in an animal before but it was so quick, and he got back to standing so quickly, that I determined it was his just his aches and pains giving him trouble and that he was fine. Strange the things we can come to believe in the face of fear. Strange how quickly we can move up and down the scale of emotions within milliseconds, each degree like a hot coal under our frightened feet.

Unfortunately, a few weeks on and it became obvious it wasn't so benign. Harleigh had another episode; one we concluded to be his thyroid. He had hypothyroidism for about a year now. So we increased his medication in an attempt to reduce, if not eliminate the seizures altogether. But this was not to be the case. Some days were better than others and I have no knowledge as to why that was but they were few and far between. Until one morning, he had a full-on seizure and lost control of his little body completely. We still tried to blame the thyroid on it. But after a few days and some wretched cluster seizures, he was off to the emergency. And he never left.

You see, it wasn't Harleigh's thyroid, his joints, his hips, his butt, his hernia, his neck, or any other part of his body that was causing his episodes. It was his heart. His heart was having trouble keeping up with his life and nobody had caught this. His rhythms were out of sync and it appeared his heart was almost stopping each time, causing a seizure-like episode. That night in the emergency room they couldn't get his heart to cooperate – it had done all it could. Early the next morning I got a call from the veterinarian saying I should make my way there now. My heart ricocheted into a fixed and locked position once more.

Strong. Strong. Strong I told myself, as my pulse without any hesitation whatsoever, threw itself in an almost suicidal fashion onto the railways tracks of my heart.

As I dashed into the clinic and was taken to him, the air awash with the aroma of panic and disinfectant, Harleigh had just finished having what was determined to be a stroke during his final episode. With no fuss, I felt the earth solidify under my feet, the most stable I had felt in weeks which allowed me make the final decision in his big life – the one where I would let my *Little Man* leave this world of pain, confusion and noise.

Moved into a private room, having a few minutes alone with him, not wanting to extend his discomfort for my imagined one, I called the doctor in and gave the sign. The sign whereby Harleigh flew like gold dust on the wings of angels right out of this world and onto the next. *Go Harleigh. Go fly with the angels. Go high. Go free. Go with my love. It's ok now. It's ok. No more pain, I promise. No more.*

The moment his spirit left his body, I could feel it arc right through the middle of mine like a missile-guided silver cord, up into my heart and out of the top of my head. Harleigh had given me one last goodbye with his entire spirit. It was so huge I thought I would pass out. I inhaled him right into my DNA and beyond and exhaled him into the canine ether of the afterlife. And just like that, he was gone. Pad, pad.

I'm still in shock, gutted to my core. My *Little Man* was supposed to still be here for many more years. I don't understand his early departure but I'm trying to make sense of it. That's just who I am. Part of me thinks he left because, if he hadn't, I might never have gone to that appointment with the cardiologist for Juno. He told me Juno's heart was having a tough time and that he may not be here much longer either. So now I am committed to doing all I can for him with medication and love. He's already doing better, now that I know. Now that I know. But still I miss the smell of pee around the house. Odd the things that wreck us.

Harleigh took up all my time. I didn't mind. I catered to his every whim knowing they weren't whims at all. He was one determined little chap, who despite all his aches and pains and surgeries, never complained but kept on going through it all like a fuzzy brown Chihuahua-dozer. Nothing was going to come between him and his food and me. Nothing. He would bite the face off anyone who tried, and truth be told, he did. He saw me through the worst and best times of the past seven years and only bit my face off a few times in the process.

He ate better than I did and he consumed everything I put in front of him. He had a love affair with chocolate and one chocolate croissant in particular. He could have eaten himself into the next dimension. God knows he tried. He drove me to the depths of pure, undiluted frustration and to the heights of great joy and every single emotion in-between. We were like old war buddies, blasting each other up and down the Richter scale of emotions. Yet, he had a sense to him that I am now coming to understand.

Like a schoolgirl tries to remember her math tables, I am just as determined to remember every single moment of time with him. And I think that in remembering I will keep his scent with me for a few days longer. I know life will dilute his memory, time will bleach it to a more transparent one to be filed away with the others who have gone before him. But before that happens, I will pull back each day with him and inhale it, moment by moment, like a rare perfume made only for me. And in doing so, I fondly remembered one day a few months back when I had been searching for a home for myself – wanting to start a new chapter in my life and finding the most perfect of houses. After the move in, boxes stacked in rooms, animals all in and counted for, in ark-like-fashion, Harleigh circled in the garden as he always did and collapsed in an exhausted repose as if to say, finally, I got her here. It's done.

I kept his little body at home for a few days and laid him out – allowing Juno and Orlagh, "new kitty" to say goodbye. But it was really for me, so I could still see him around the house, so I could light a daily candle, play music, cry uncontrollably into the gray couch and the navy night, not caring if I ever recovered from such a cry. Why did Harleigh leave? Did he have his exit date already planned? Was his contract up? Maybe Harleigh just got tired of wearing his clothes. They didn't fit him anyway and what's a life with so much pain?

Well, whatever the answer, it certainly won't bring me any comfort right now. Because his absence sits in my chest like a bowling ball, demolishing everything inside, slaying my bits and pieces to bits and pieces. I know healing lies within the minutes, the hours, the days; that bastard time whose only job is to diminish the pain, not allowing us to bend our mind so easily backward to the past, so the pain can subside with each insufficient bend. But until that is done, I'm still bending backwards.

Harleigh
Addendum

The day after I finished this story about Harleigh, I had a reading with my good friend Lisa. She's read all my animals many times and the readings have brought me so much insight and laughter and helped me deepen my bond with them. She called ahead of our scheduled time and said that Harleigh was ready to go. I expected nothing less from the *Little Man.*

Harleigh told me a lot during the reading, and I do feel the need to keep most of it between us two. But for the purpose of this book, I wanted to share some of it which highlights the ability of animals, even in the afterlife, to continue to express their deep love and gratitude for their experience here on earth and those they have loved along the way.

Lisa did tell me Harleigh was enjoying being free of his body and that everything happened the way it was supposed to. He had felt little pain in his final hours. That brought me instant comfort. I needed to know that more than anything. It's every

Mother's wish, I'd imagine. Harleigh went onto explain that one of the great lessons he learned in this lifetime was that real power in life comes from within. It comes from how we present ourselves, not from what we do, and rarely from what we say. He definitely showed me that every day of his life. Through the reading itself, I was able to let go of wanting to have a sign from him because here I was chatting away as though he hadn't really left – just nudged closer to my soul and intertwined himself forever in my heart.

Finally, as we were saying our goodbyes, knowing they weren't really goodbyes at all, Harleigh showed Lisa a peacock. She asked what it meant to me and I wasn't able to figure it out at that moment but I knew there was most likely something to it. So after hanging up the phone with Lisa, I looked at Juno and said, *"Hey Juno, what does a peacock mean to you?"* He tilted his tan, graying head to the side and probably wondered a bit more about my growing stupidity and looked at me as if to say, Duh Mum, don't you remember why you named me Juno?

And there it was like a blazing sun over my dumb Irish head – I had named him Juno after the Irish play *Juno and The Paycock*, by Sean O'Casey.

At that moment I could hear Harleigh say, "Focus, focus on what is right in front of you, it's a gift; life's a gift, unwrap it every day like the present it is, and should there be a chocolate croissant in it also, well that wouldn't be a bad thing either."

Tip-tap

You tip-tapped on my wooden floors
Like drops of salvation within my broken heart
This heart you came here to mend
And mend you did

Gargantuan although the task
Your soul knew no limits
It left your body behind
Too much earth for Little Man
Too much

Why did you leave so soon?
I wasn't ready
I would never have been ready for such a blow
My heart is less than paper thin now
Stretched to its limits

I fail to comprehend any of it
Wicked loss has once more cut my soul asunder
Your bed lies scathingly empty
The blasting wind has come to carry you home
And I left here blown to bloody pieces

I look for you at night
I listen for your breath
I was aware of your every move
Even while I slept

Oh sweet, sweet Little Man
These days are dirty
This life is for the lost

The Art of Embracing Pain

I have lived in America for over two decades now, and during that time I've made many the emergency plane ride home for funerals and it's something I'd be happy to never do again. It's desperate. It brings a whole other dimension to losing somebody we love and the intricate aftermath. The deaths of parents in particular, can blast a deeply introspective light on the decision to leave in the first place. And the price one pays for enjoying that luxury up until it no longer feels like a luxury, but the burden of all burdens, is the one sin no amount of confessions can ever take away. But as I have said before, that's for a different book entirely.

A good death can take many forms, and being open to them and embracing the possibilities that present themselves, can be an art in itself. Not being able to hasten or postpone death is the gift, although at the time when we are in the trenches of the dying process itself for humans or animals, it might not seem like such a blessed event. If we could just adjust our way of thinking before the time approaches, we might have a better chance at seeing the beauty reflecting back at us in the face of a good death. That is my wish for every living creature on this planet.

When we have lost a loved one, healing knows no clock and grief has no expiration date. But if we try to reach beyond our own imagined limited capabilities into the pure essence of being, we will find what it is we need and what never, ever gets left behind; that simply boils down to love, however immature or lacking edge that might sound. Ninety-nine percent of life will boil off to be waste material, junk that will float to the top that we can dump overboard – where all that will be left is love. It is the thin thread of our existence that weathers all storms of the heart and every battle of the soul. It never, ever dies. It's not to say aches won't ever leave or should, but there will remain the memory of life to wrap them in, a comfrey salve for the forget-me-not memories of a much-lived-life.

I have learned through the years, it is a wicked insult in the face of loss and pain to not try and grow beyond it. To not let it have its way with us and to lean into the very thing that causes our hearts to break open. It is no ordinary art this embracing pain. It takes a lot of work and it will come with time but one does well to remember the pain of not moving beyond it. And the day will come when the risk of remaining the same becomes more painful than the risk of bloom.

Over the years I have found grief to be the purest emotion of them all. Grieving is one of the most natural things I have ever done. I could assume that it might be my default emotion like some people might have insecurity as theirs – or the myriad of others which exist or that we create.

But whatever the nature of my comfort with grief, it matters not. What does matter is that I can feel it and maybe because it feels so natural, maybe that is in itself a sign that I've got a bucket load of it to empty out – because as I child I held it all in, mine and my Mother's. It was a gargantuan job which the most empathetic child takes on. I did it at a deep cellular level, the deepest level that vibrates at the same frequency of love, because that is what I thought love was. It is an old image of myself that needs much help in the dismantling. But as I continue to do so, I can tell anyone, and I will, that nobody out there holds the answers to our grief – not one person. And nobody can tell you how to grieve.

We must follow that voice inside our hearts which blasts the way through the concrete of pain and follow it to its conclusion, transforming the smithereens of solace into a deeper and more profound knowledge of the workings of the human heart. By doing so, we will be guided to enter each phase of fear with no idea if we will ever return – and that's alright. It's in the not-knowing that we will be known, as we break down the walls of half-truths, untruths and out-dated images of ourselves, and move into the fire of no-holding-back.

Odd thing worth noting for myself and I will, is that in all of this sadness, I've felt that if I just let it in, followed it to its conclusion, not knowing where that really was, but having an idea it might be at the epicenter of the origin of my ache – that I would heal, but not a moment before. And even more odd, when I've emerged from each loss, I've noticed I've never felt more raw and alive, untouchable at times for fear I might electrify somebody with my sensitivity, but shockingly alive. And at that precise moment, that moment when it felt like the dark was going to obliterate the light, it failed. I call that healing and nobody can tell me any different as I look down towards my insides and feel my heart still hanging around like an abused hammock between my ribs, swaying back and forth with each blow.

Yet I'll be brutally honest and say that some days I just inhabit the space between whats happened and what could happen. I call this place fear. I call this place anxiety. I call this place madness. There is little I can do about it except survive and feel the insanity, and know with an equally fanatical certainty it will come to pass, not disappear. It will pass just long enough to regain my balance and find my way back into life once more, comfortably uncertain about one more go around, one more dance with this thing called grief.

Throughout it all, I've tried not to underestimate the signs in nature, music, smells, memory, dreams and even random encounters with strangers during a time of grief and loss. I do believe nothing is random, not a blessed thing, and that there are lessons in every second which dwell in the moments that are interwoven with the language of the heart. Signs from the spirit world, source, God, loved ones who have passed, animals who are waiting for us and beyond – is the glue that can be pasted into the crevices of a breaking heart until it heals. These signs can become an invisible tourniquet for the healing soul for those who are left behind, piecing the pieces of their lives together until there are no more pieces, only pictures of brilliant memories that we shared with those we loved in a period of time that can be brought back into focus, if we just close our eyes and exhale their name.

In love and light

Elizabeth

Paradise Row

You have to be prepared to allow yourself to disappear
To allow something greater than yourself emerge
From the banality of the perception of who you think you are
Something great has to work its way through you
We are the vehicles for simple messages
In amazing formats
In delightful prose

If we stood back and watched ourselves
We'd find it incredibly erotic
We would ignite within
Turned on by our very existence
Watching ourselves emerge

What if we were perfect
from day one?
What if nothing needed changing,
Rearranging or
Solutions?
As the nips and tucks of our personality only served to
Disassemble our greatness
One slammed door at a time.

The greatest illusion is time.
We think we have much
Then we feel we have little
Then we are out of it
What would more of it give us;
The ability to be right?

This is my life
And I am in deep
Was there any other way?

I cross a street and read the sign;
"Paradise Row"
Everything can now wait
Down it I must go

Let nothing change.
Let everything be still,
For within this stillness
we remain to be seen

Being misunderstood
Allows me to understand
What I have done wrong
I should have concerned myself with myself

It is a thin veil of apprehension
That doesn't allow me fully see
What flocks beside me
Momentarily I abandon the pain
And my spirit
Myself are unrestrained – free

You and I
We are not of this place
This is life for now
And we are in deep
And the truth shall surface
As nothing else remains to be seen
We seize the pain
And the joy seizes us;
Incomprehensible human decay
While the flesh only follows the mind
Chewing one limb, one cell at a time

The rules are that there are none
We will die finding a category to fit in
My life in italics is still my life
Medium rare and slightly salted

Beware of the myth of yourself
It can swallow you whole
Choose everything well and
Be a bridge back to yourself
Become whole

If my love hurt you
Forgive me
It was good intention gone awry
Muteless at times
dissolving into the navy night
Crippled by my emotions
I slammed right through your ribs
While trying to reach for your heart
For in that knot of fire
I knew I would find home

~ Life, it has been simply delightful to make your acquaintance ~

Made in the USA
San Bernardino, CA
22 December 2017